WHAT'S FOR LUNCH?

Dairy

Honor Head

QED Publishing

Copyright © QED Publishing 2006

First published in the UK in 2006 by
QED Publishing
A Quarto Group company
226 City Road
London EC1V 2TT
www.qed-publishing.co.uk

A Catalogue record for this book is available from the British Library.

ISBN 1 84538 372 9

Written by Honor Head
Designed by Danny Pyne
Edited by Hannah Ray and Barbara Bourassa
Consultancy by Roy Balam and Sarah Schenker of the British Nutrition Foundation
Photographer Michael Wicks
Illustrations by Bill Greenhead

Publisher Steve Evans
Art Director Zeta Davies
Editorial Director Jean Coppendale

Printed and bound in China

Picture credits
Key: t = top, b = bottom, c = centre, l = left, r = right, FC = front cover

Creative image library/Greg Cuddiford 8l; **Corbis**/Envision 26cl/
A.Inden/zefa 18/ Photocuisine 27br/ Christoph Wilhelm 23tr; **Dorling Kindersley**/8r;
FLPA/Nick Spurling 9cr; **Getty Images**/Tim Flach 6, 9tl/ GK Hart/Vikki Hart 8c/
StockFood Creative Chris Alack 27cl/ StockFood Creative William Lingford 26br/
StockFood Creative Joris Luyten 26tr/ PicturePress FC.

Before undertaking any activity which involves eating or the preparation of food,
always check whether the children in your care have any food allergies. In a
classroom situation, prior written permission from parents may be required.

Website information is correct at time of going to press. However, the publishers
cannot accept liability for any information or links found on third-party websites.

Words in **bold** can be found in the glossary on page 30.

Contents

In the mix

Eating a mix of different types of food is the best way to keep our bodies fit and healthy. Having the right mix of foods is called eating a balanced diet, but what does this mean?

Balanced vs. unbalanced

Do you know someone who eats mostly cakes, crisps and sweets? That's an example of an unbalanced diet because it is made up mainly of one type of food. All types of food can be put into one of five groups. To eat a balanced diet you need to eat foods from all five groups. This is because one type of food on its own cannot provide your body with everything it needs to grow and stay strong and healthy.

What's in which group?

- **Milk and dairy foods**
  This group contains foods such as milk, cheese and yoghurt.
- **Bread, other cereals and potatoes**
  Sweet potatoes, rice and noodles are all part of this group.
- **Foods that contain fat or sugar**
  Cakes, sweets, butter and mayonnaise are all included in this group.

- **Meat, fish and alternatives**
  This group contains foods such as tuna, chicken and beef as well as foods with lots of **protein**, for example eggs and tofu.
- **Fruit and vegetables**
  Fresh, canned and frozen fruit and veggies are all in this group, as are 100 per cent fruit or vegetable juices.

Getting it right

bread, other cereals and potatoes

fruit and vegetables

meat, fish and alternatives

foods that contain fats and sugars

milk and dairy foods

Some foods are better for you than others. For example, your body needs more fruit and vegetables than foods that contain fats and sugars. This means that you need to eat more food from some of the groups than from others. To help you remember the amount of each type of food your body needs, take a look at the plate above.

Perfect plate

To stay super healthy, you should make sure that about a third of what you eat is made up of fruit and vegetables. Another third of your diet should be from the bread, cereals and potatoes group, while the final third is made up of a mix of the other three food groups (dairy foods, meat, fish and alternatives, and foods that contain sugar or fat). So, think of your food in thirds – it's easy!

Weblink
Some countries, such as the USA and Australia, use a special food pyramid to help explain how to eat a healthy and balanced diet. To find out more, visit www.mypyramid.gov/kids

Dairy delight

This book is all about foods from the dairy group. Milk, cream, butter, yoghurt and cheese are all types of dairy food. All of these foods are made from milk, but why are they called dairy foods?

Milk made

Milk comes from cows and cows are kept on a dairy farm, which is why foods made from milk are called dairy foods. The cows are milked twice a day and the milk is either bottled or is used to make cheese, butter or other dairy products.

Superfood!

Eating the right amount of foods from this group helps towards giving us the **vitamins**, **minerals** and proteins that we need to keep our bodies healthy, to grow strong, to keep our brains working (essential for homework!) and to keep our skin and hair looking good. Milk is one of nature's superfoods, and is especially good for growing children – and that's you!

Milk's a must

Milk, and most foods made from milk, contains **calcium**, which help you to grow strong teeth and bones. Without the right amount of calcium, your teeth would not develop properly and your bones could break easily. This is a disease known as rickets. So drink up and keep those teeth and bones in tip-top condition!

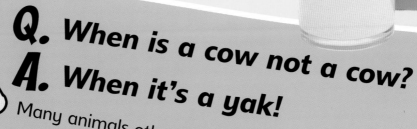

Q. When is a cow not a cow?
A. When it's a yak!

Many animals other than cows can supply us with milk. These animals include sheep, goats, camels, water buffalo and even yaks. Yaks are large cattle that live in Tibet. They have long, shaggy hair and their milk is pink!

Cream

It's no wonder cats love cream – it's delicious! There are lots of different sorts of cream in the shops: **clotted cream**, whipping cream, single cream and double cream. However, cream contains fat, so it's best to only have it now and again, and not to have too much!

We all scream for ice cream

Ice cream is made from the layer of cream found on the top of milk. This cream is mixed with sugar and other flavourings. Ice cream is a really yummy once-in-a-while treat. What's your favourite flavour?

7

The milky way

Milk comes in many different forms,
but it usually starts with a cow.

Weblink
To find out more
about dairy cows
and milk, visit
www.moomilk.com

Heard about the herd?

We all know that most milk comes from cows, but
did you know that there are lots of different types
of cow? Here are just a few:

Friesian

Guernsey

Jersey

Different cows give different types and amounts of milk.
Friesian cows give the most milk and Jersey cows give
the least. Some cows give over 18 litres of milk each
day – that's enough for more than 100 glasses!

From the cows to the shops

This is how milk gets from the cow to a carton on the supermarket shelf.

① Milking machines

In the past, cows used to be milked by hand. Today, big dairy herds are milked by machine. Some farms can milk up to 500 cows twice a day!

② Tanker deliveries

The fresh milk is put into huge, refrigerated tankers which keep it cool and make sure it stays fresh. The tankers take the milk to a **processing plant**, where it is **pasteurized** and **processed** to make it safe to drink.

③ Milk and more

From the processing plant, the milk is either put into cartons or bottles, or it is sent to other factories where it is made into cheese, yoghurt and other dairy products. These are then taken to the supermarket for us to buy.

GROSS!

The taste of a cow's milk depends on what she eats. Cows are fed hay to keep their milk tasting sweet. If a cow was fed cabbage, her milk would taste of cabbages!

Bite size

Milk straight from the cow contains **bacteria** that can make humans ill. If the milk is heated to a certain temperature, the germs are killed – this is called pasteurization.

Lunch choice

Try this fun lunch with some of your friends. It's easy to eat at the table or as a picnic.

Cheese please!

Why not team up with some friends and each bring in a different cheese. You can have your own cheese tasting – very grown up!

Cheese platter

Brown roll

Pickle

Fruit salad

Choose cheese

If you have cheese in a sandwich or roll, add some sliced tomatoes, lettuce, cucumber or onion. Try different cheeses in your sandwich, such as Edam, Red Leicester and Emmental.

Snack attack

Here are some ideas for other cheesy lunchbox options:

Cheese kebabs

Thread cubes of cheese onto cocktail sticks with some cherry tomatoes, cubes of cucumber, pieces of raw pepper, raw button mushrooms and cubes of canned pineapple.

Bottle of water

Mixed salad

Cheese bundles

Cut sticks of your favourite hard cheese. Mix with sticks of cucumber and wrap up the bundles in slices of ham to make tasty parcels.

Cheese-topped salad

Having a salad? Why not sprinkle some grated cheese on top. Delicious!

Wedges of cheese

The simple choice

Nothing beats a chunk of cheese, an apple and a brown roll for a lunch that's quick to pack and easy to eat.

Cheese board

There are loads of different types of cheese. Some are firm, while others are soft enough to spread. Which cheeses have you tasted?

Hard cheese

Hard cheeses include Edam, Gouda, Cheddar and Red Leicester. These are the cheeses you can slice to go in a sandwich, grate to put in salads or sprinkle over baked beans on toast.

Gouda

Cheddar

Edam

Emmenthal

Red Leicester

Stilton

Soft cheese

These are the squidgy cheeses with difficult names like Brie, Mozzarella, Camembert and Dolcelatte. These cheeses are often spread on crackers, rolls or bread. Mozzarella is often used on pizzas.

Brie

Camembert

Mozzarella

Even more cheese!

Two other types of soft cheese are Feta cheese and goats' cheese. Feta cheese is made from sheep or goats' milk. It is salty and is used in Greek salads. Goats' cheese is made from goats' milk and can be baked, fried or spread on crackers or bread. It has a strong taste.

Feta

Q. When is cheese not cheese?
A. When it's a piece of cake!

Cheesecake is a delicious cake made from, you guessed it... cheese! Cream cheese is mixed with sugar and poured onto a base made from crushed wheatmeal biscuits. It is then chilled in the fridge for several hours. A fruit topping is often added.

Dolcelatte

Weblink
Find out about different cheeses from around the world at www.cheese.com/country.asp

Bite size
The reason some cheeses, such as Stilton, are blue is because they have been injected with a special **mould**. This mould is safe to eat and the cheeses are strong tasting and delicious!

How cheese is made...

There are thousands of different types of cheese, but all cheese is made from milk, whether it comes from a cow, a goat or even a camel!

Making soft cheese

A special bacteria, called a starter, is added to the milk to start it **fermenting**.

The milk is poured into a vat and warmed.

Then something called **rennet** is added. This makes the milk turn into semi-solid lumps. These lumps are called curds. At this stage, most soft cheeses, such as cottage cheese and cream cheese, are nearly finished.

The soft cheeses are then packaged and sent to the shops, ready to sell.

Making hard cheese

Curds and whey

Can you remember what little Miss Muffet was eating in the nursery rhyme? Curds are the semi-solid lumps that make soft cheese. Whey is the white, milky liquid that is drained off the curds before they are turned into hard cheese.

1 To make hard cheese, the curds are cut, stirred and heated to help remove any liquid (the whey).

2 The cheese is salted, then poured into a **mould**.

3 The mould is **pressed** to make sure most of the liquid is squeezed out.

Depending on the type of cheese, it is then left to form a rind, dipped in wax, pressed again or injected with bacteria.

4

It's a wrap!

Brie is left to form a rind. The rind is safe to eat.

Edam cheese is made in a round mould and then dipped in red wax. The wax needs to be peeled off before you can eat the cheese.

Cheddar is made by wrapping it in a huge cloth, keeping it pressed and allowing it to age.

Lunch choice

Cottage cheese is a great choice for lunch. It's full of calcium, is low in fat and goes with almost anything!

Side salad

Cottage cheese, peppers and sweetcorn

Pitta pocket

Creamy cheese

Cottage cheese is a soft white cheese with a mild flavour. It is made from cheese curds which have been drained but not pressed, so some of the whey remains. You can eat cottage cheese straight from the tub but it tastes great when mixed with salad vegetables, such as red and green peppers and sweetcorn. Mix it up and use it as a filling for a pitta pocket. Bet you can't wait until lunchtime to tuck in!

Fab with fruit

Cottage cheese also goes really well with fruit. Try mixing it with some pineapple chunks and grapes, or with cubes of apple and some raisins.

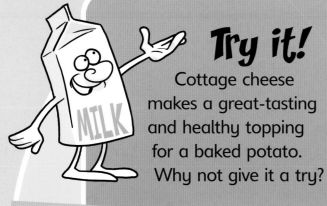

Try it!

Cottage cheese makes a great-tasting and healthy topping for a baked potato. Why not give it a try?

Delicious dip

Either on its own or mixed with chopped spring onions or chives, cottage cheese makes a yummy lunchtime dip. Spoon it into a tub, snap on the lid and add it to your lunchbox. Low-fat nachos or carrot and celery sticks make the perfect dippers.

Water

Satsuma

Check it out

Queso blanco (Spanish for white cheese) is a creamy, soft cheese that is made by pressing the whey from cottage cheese. It is used to top Mexican dishes such as enchiladas (filled tortilla flatbreads that are baked in the oven) and is also used as a filling in quesadillas (a folded tortilla that is filled with cheese and then fried or toasted to make the cheese melt).

Yell for yoghurt

A good source of calcium, protein and B vitamins, yoghurt comes in lots of different flavours and types, and is a great choice for your lunchbox.

It's alive!

Yoghurt is made by fermenting milk. 'Friendly' bacteria is added to the milk which changes it into a thicker substance with more tangy taste. Live, or natural, yoghurt contains the friendly bacteria. Sometimes yoghurt is pasteurized so that it lasts longer. Pasteurizing the yoghurt kills the bacteria. As well as plain yoghurts, you can buy all sorts of flavoured yoghurts, from fruit flavours such as apricot and strawberry, to chocolate and toffee.

Try it!

Yoghurt tastes really good when it is poured over breakfast cereal. Why not try it as a healthy and tasty start to your day?

Bacteria buddies

The friendly bacteria found in yoghurt are good for your body. They are different from the type of bacteria that can make you ill. Friendly bacteria help to keep your digestive system healthy and working properly. So eat some yoghurt for your lunch and help keep your body healthy and in tip-top condition.

It's how old?

Yoghurt has been around for nearly 5000 years. It is thought that it used to be made by fermenting milk in a goat-skin sack. Nowadays it is made in factories and you can buy it in the shops, so no need for the goat-skin bag!

Say yes to yoghurt

Yoghurt is available in lots of different forms. Small pots are perfect for popping into your lunchbox, as are squeezable tubes. If you have large containers of yoghurt at home, spoon some into a smaller tub with some chopped fruit, nuts or sunflower seeds and drizzle some honey over the top for a fantastic lunchtime pudding.

Weblink

Visit www.cspinet.org /smartmouth/recipes_articles and click on 'Fruit smoothies' to get some ideas for fab smoothies using yoghurt.

Bite size

Frozen yoghurt is similar to ice cream, but is made by freezing yoghurt instead of cream. Frozen yoghurt is lower in fat than ice cream.

Lunch choice

Rice pudding

The perfect way to add to your daily intake of dairy? Have it as a pudding or a playground snack.

Fruit juice

Banana

Rice pudding with fruit

Rice for pudding!

The rice you get in a rice pudding is a different type from the rice you use for **savoury** foods. Rice pudding is made with rice, milk and a little sugar, and is a good source of calcium. You can buy it ready made in tubs or cans and, to make it extra tasty, you could add some of your favourite fruits and nuts. Why not try...

Strawberries

Blueberries

Raspberries

Chopped nuts

Peach

Raisins

Custard

Custard is another type of dairy dessert. It is made with eggs and sugar with milk or cream. It is often warmed up and poured over hot desserts, such as sticky toffee pudding, but it tastes great cold, too. You can buy custard ready made in cartons. Pour some into a small tub and stir in some sliced bananas. Perfect for your lunchbox!

Sandwiches

Summer fruits

CHECK IT OUT!

There are lots of milk-based puddings available in tubs. These are really handy for school lunches but check that they don't contain too much sugar. Look out for 'low fat' or 'no added sugar' on the label.

Try it!

Chocolate bars, cream cakes and tubs of ice cream are not ideal lunchtime snacks. Eat them as a treat only, as part of a balanced diet.

Drink up!

You can drink milk in many different ways: hot or cold, plain or flavoured, or even with ice cubes.

Make mine milk

Milk is the first food we ever have and is essential for healthy growth. On a winter's day, a cup of milky hot chocolate from a thermos flask will warm you up, and a long, chilled glass of milk will keep you cool in summer. Perfect!

CHECK IT OUT!

Bored with milk that tastes like plain old milk? Why not add a dash of chocolate or fruit syrup for a really yummy milk drink. Simply stir in the syrup and slurp away!

Tutti frutti!

Milkshakes are a fun drink. You could make a fruit smoothie in the morning, pop it in a Thermos and sip it throughout the day. You can make smoothies by adding your favourite fruit to milk or yoghurt and blending it together until it becomes a smooth liquid. Add some water if your smoothie is too thick. Try adding a handful of strawberries or raspberries to your milkshake for extra vitamins.

Indian milkshake

Lassi is a milk drink that comes from India. A sweet lassi is made from yoghurt and water mixed with some sugar and a pinch of salt. The salty version is made with milk and yoghurt, cumin seeds, salt and lemon or mint. Fruit lassis are mixed with crushed mangoes and pineapples. Yum!

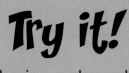

Try it!

If you are buying ready-made milkshakes or smoothies, check out the label for added sugar and fats. It's best to make your own if you can.

Dairy diet alert!

Some people can't have dairy milk because they have an **allergy** to it. This means it makes them ill.

Not for me, thanks!

A small number of people are allergic to milk from cows and food made with cows' milk. This means that their bodies reject the milk when they eat or drink it, and they become ill. They cannot eat or drink anything that contains cows' milk, such as cheese, yoghurt or milk chocolate.

Cows are so yesterday!

Milk substitutes

There are lots of other types of milk for people who cannot drink cows' milk. These include soya milk, almond milk, coconut milk and oat milk. Some people who cannot drink cows' milk are able to drink milk that comes from goats or sheep.

Super soya

Soya milk is made from soya beans. It is a good source of protein, and often has vitamins and minerals added, too. Soya milk can be used in many of the same ways that cows' milk is used, such as for making cheese, pouring over your cereal or in cooking.

Top up

People who are told by their doctors to avoid cows' milk can eat the following foods to get plenty of calcium:

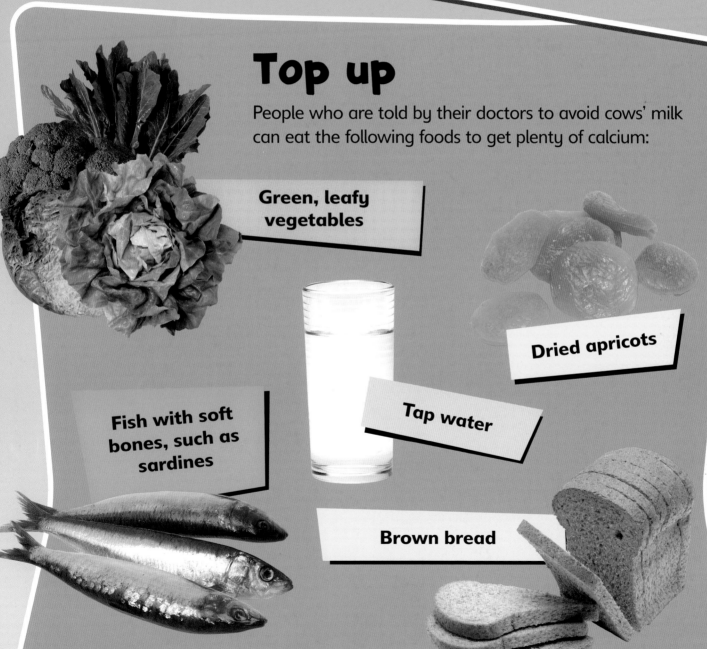

Green, leafy vegetables

Dried apricots

Tap water

Fish with soft bones, such as sardines

Brown bread

Pinboard

Pick a postcard to see how dairy foods are eaten in other countries...

Greece

Greek yoghurt is very rich and is eaten with honey for breakfast in Greece.

Wales

Welsh rarebit is melted cheese on toast with added mustard and seasonings.

India

Paneer is a type of soft Indian cheese used with vegetables. It can also be wrapped in dough and deep fried.

Turkey

Ayran is a popular drink in Turkey. It is made from yoghurt and water, and sometimes has salt or chopped mint added for flavour – a bit like an Indian lassi.

Switzerland

Cheese fondue is a favourite in Switzerland. Pieces of bread and potato are dipped into a bowl of melted cheese.

France

Crème brûlée is eaten as a dessert in France. It is a rich custard topped with a layer of hard caramel, made by burning sugar.

Quiz time

Multiple-choice

1. Which of the following should be eaten as a treat?
a. skimmed milk
b. frozen yoghurt
c. clotted cream
d. cottage cheese

2. Why are dairy foods good for you?
a. they contain calcium
b. they contain vitamins
c. they contain protein
d. all of the above

3. Which of the following is not a dairy product?
a. coconut milk
b. yoghurt
c. rice pudding
d. double cream

4. Which of the following is not a type of hard cheese?
a. Stilton
b. Edam
c. Emmanthal
d. Dolcelatte

5. Which of the following is not a type of soft cheese?
a. Mozzarella
b. Cheddar
c. Camembert
d. Cottage cheese

Match the food with the word that best describes it

milk

hard cheese

frozen

dairy alternative

ice cream

Cheddar

Brie

drink

soft cheese

soya milk

True or false?

1. Crème brûlée is a type of cheese.
2. Some people are allergic to milk.
3. Cheese can be made from soya milk.
4. The rind on Brie cheese is safe to eat.
5. Clotted cream is low in fat.
6. Cottage cheese tastes good with fruit.
7. A lassi is an Australian milkshake.
8. Milk can be made from almonds.
9. Paneer is a cheese from Switzerland.
10. Custard can not be eaten cold.

What's the answer?

1. Are some dairy foods better for you than others?
2. Why is calcium important for children?
3. What should you do if you are allergic to cow's milk?
4. Can you plan a lunchbox menu for a week so that each day contains a different type of dairy food?
5. What percentage of your diet should be made up of foods from the dairy group?

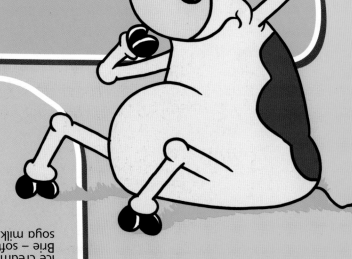

Answers

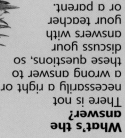

True or false?
1. FALSE
2. TRUE
3. TRUE
4. TRUE
5. FALSE
6. TRUE
7. FALSE
8. TRUE
9. FALSE
10. FALSE

Match the food with the word that best describes it
milk – drink
Cheddar – hard cheese
ice cream – frozen
Brie – soft cheese
soya milk – dairy alternative

Multiple choice
1. c – clotted cream
2. d – all of the above
3. a – coconut milk
4. d – Dolcelatte
5. b – Cheddar

What's the answer?
There is not necessarily a right or a wrong answer to these questions, so discuss your answers with your teacher or a parent.

Glossary

allergy when a person has an allergy to a certain type of food, such as nuts or milk, it means that eating the food makes them ill. For example, people with a nut allergy might have difficulty breathing or get a rash after eating nuts

bacteria tiny living things that are invisible to the human eye. Some bacteria is bad for us, and can make us ill. However, other types of bacteria can help our digestion and is good for us

calcium a mineral found in dairy food that helps to build strong teeth and bones

clotted cream this is a very thick cream which has a lot of fat in it

fermenting changing a food from one thing to another by adding a substance, such as rennet, to the original food or drink

minerals substances found in certain foods we eat that keep our bodies healthy, such as calcium, which helps strengthen bones and teeth

mould (1) a type of fungi that grows in or on food. Most mould is bad and means the food cannot be eaten without making us ill. However, some mould is harmless and is injected into cheese to give it a certain appearance and taste

mould (2) a container in which something, such as a jelly or a cheese, is shaped or made

pasteurized this is when milk is heated to a certain temperature to kill any germs

pressed this is a process used to make some types of cheese. The cheeses are 'pressed', or squeezed, in a mould. Pressed cheeses are usually hard cheeses such as Cheddar

processed when a food has been through a series of actions to make it look different from its natural state

processing plant a factory where food is processed and packaged before being delivered to the shops

protein part of the food we eat that helps to build muscles and keep us healthy

rennet this is an ingredient used in cheesemaking which helps the milk to form solid pieces

savoury a food that is not sweet

vitamins these are found in the food we eat and are essential to help us stay healthy. There are many different vitamins, such as A, B, C and D

Index

Parents' and teachers' notes

- Talk to children about dairies. Do they know what a dairy is? Why are dairy foods called dairy foods?

- How many dairy foods can the children name?

- Are the children surprised by anything they have seen or read in the book? Can they name some of the foods that are made from milk?

- Talk about what the children plan to eat for lunch, or what they have already eaten. Did they eat any dairy foods?

- Collect pictures of lots of different foods such as bread, pies, chocolate, cakes, fruit and vegetables. Ask the children which foods contain milk.

- Discuss the dairy food available for school lunch. Do the children think the foods on offer are tasty or healthy? Do they have a favourite?

- Discuss different types of cuisine or cultures, such as Italian and Indian foods. How do they make use of dairy food? Ask the children, in groups, to research dairy foods from around the world.

- Keep a Dairy Diary. Ask the children to write down what they have to eat for lunch over the course of a week. Then ask them to write down any dairy foods that were included in their meals. Have the children eaten any dairy foods without realizing it?